Polar

Arctic Foxes

by Emily Rose Townsend

Consulting Editor: Gail Saunders-Smith, Ph.D.
Consultant: Brock R. McMillan, Ph.D.
Associate Professor, Department of Biological Sciences
Minnesota State University, Mankato

Capstone
press

Mankato, Minnesota

Pebble Books are published by Capstone Press
1710 Roe Crest Drive, North Mankato, Minnesota 56003
www.capstonepub.com

Copyright © 2004 by Capstone Press, a Capstone imprint. All rights reserved.
No part of this publication may be reproduced in whole or in part,
or stored in a retrieval system, or transmitted in any form or by any means,
electronic, mechanical, photocopying, recording, or otherwise,
without written permission of the publisher.
For information regarding permission, write to Capstone Press,
1710 Roe Crest Drive, North Mankato, Minnesota 56003.

Library of Congress Cataloging-in-Publication Data
Townsend, Emily Rose.
 Arctic foxes / by Emily Rose Townsend.
 p. cm.—(Polar animals)
 Includes bibliographical references and index.
 Contents: Arctic foxes—Where arctic foxes live—What arctic foxes do.
 ISBN-13: 978-0-7368-2356-2 (hardcover)
 ISBN-10: 0-7368-2356-5 (hardcover)
 ISBN 13: 978-0-7368-9611-5 (softcover pbk.)
 ISBN 10: 0-7368-9611-2 (softcover pbk.)
 1. Arctic fox—Juvenile literature. [1. Arctic fox. 2. Foxes.] I. Title.
QL737.C22T68 2004
599.776'4—dc21   2003011248

Note to Parents and Teachers

The Polar Animals series supports national science standards related to life science. This book describes and illustrates arctic foxes. The photographs support early readers in understanding the text. The repetition of words and phrases helps early readers learn new words. This book also introduces early readers to subject-specific vocabulary words, which are defined in the Glossary. Early readers may need assistance to read some words and to use the Table of Contents, Glossary, Read More, Internet Sites, and Index/Word List sections of the book.

Printed in the United States of America in North Mankato, Minnesota.
042013
007305R

Table of Contents

Arctic Foxes 5
Where Arctic Foxes Live. 13
What Arctic Foxes Do 17

Glossary 22
Read More 23
Internet Sites. 23
Index/Word List. 24

Arctic Foxes

Arctic foxes are mammals with thick fur and short ears.

6

Arctic foxes have long bushy tails. Their tails keep them warm when they sleep.

8

Arctic foxes have white fur in winter. Their fur is mostly brown in summer.

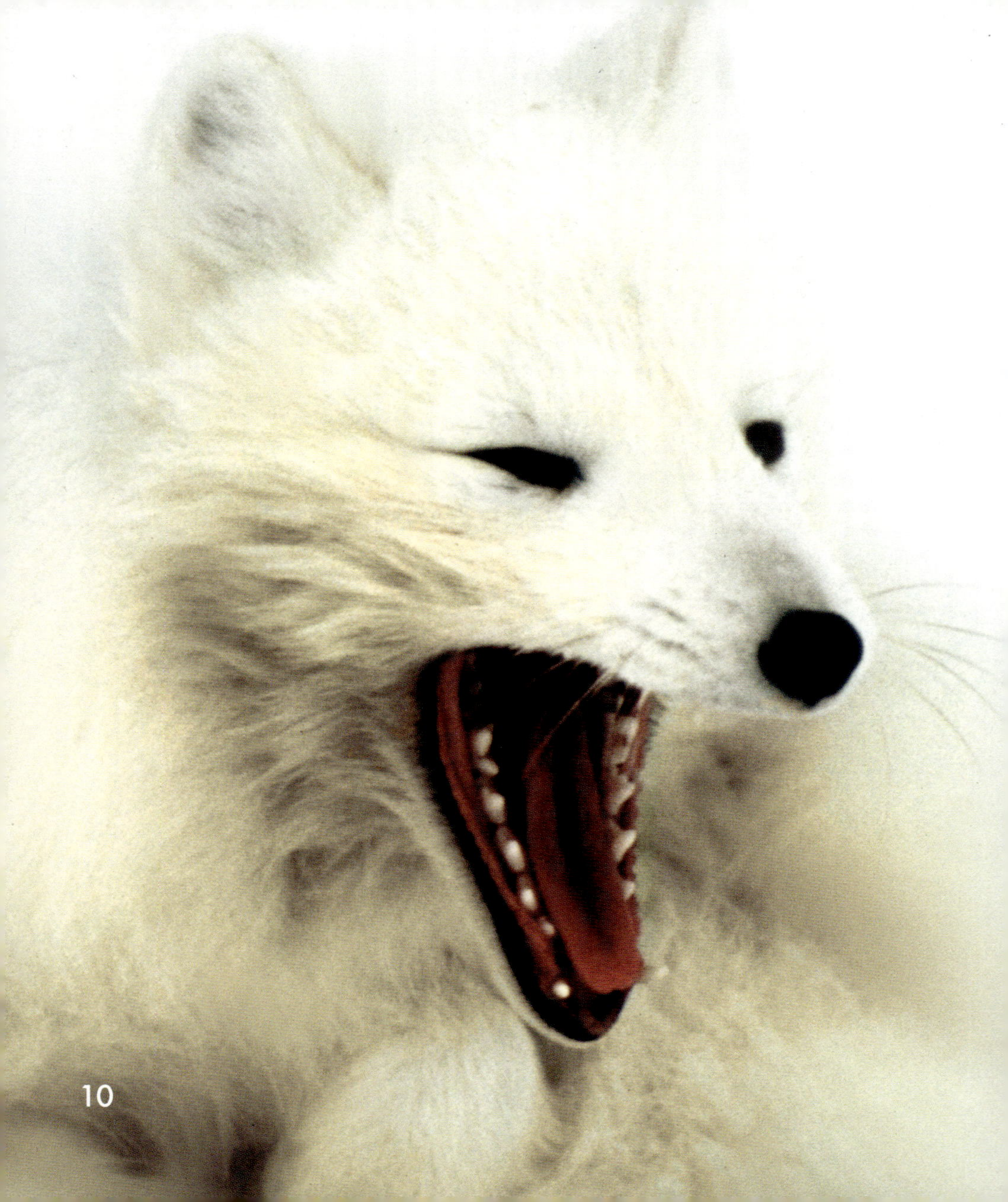

Arctic foxes
have sharp teeth
and sharp claws.

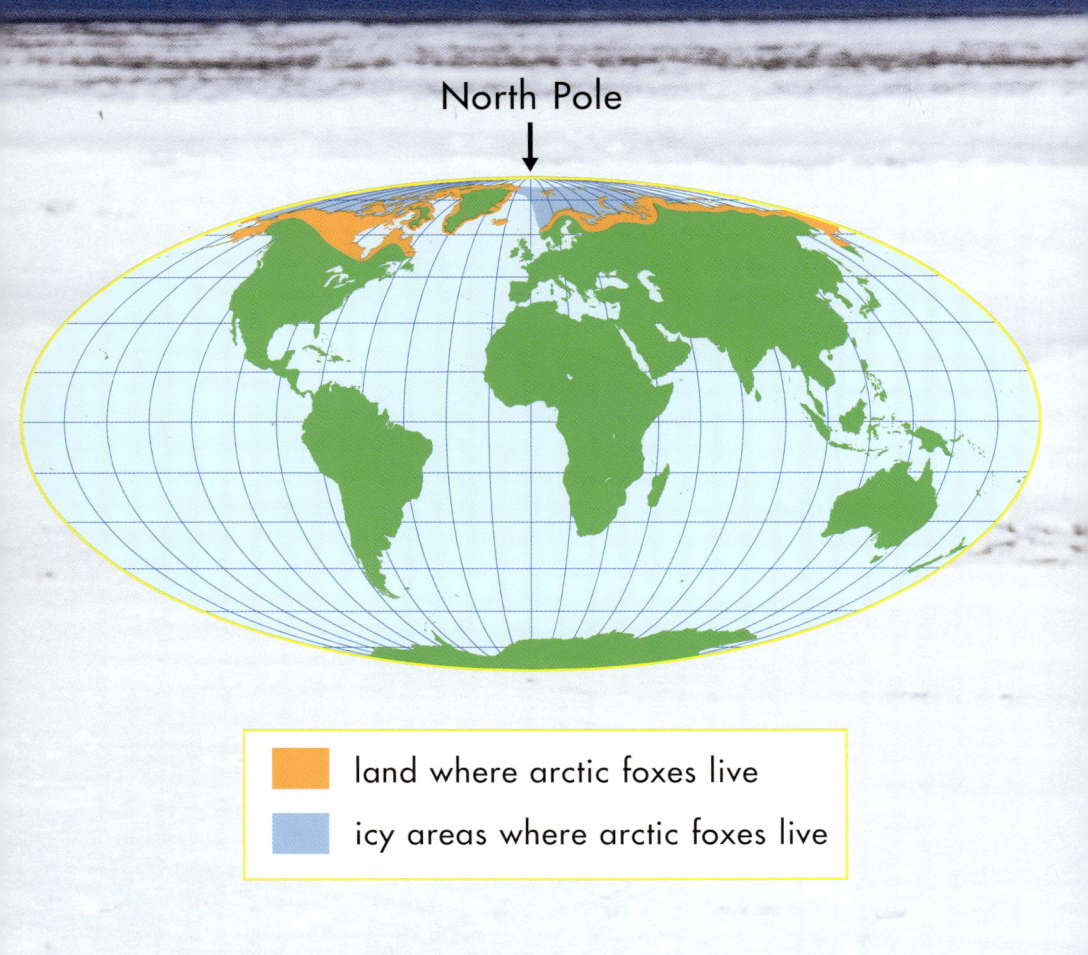

North Pole

▇ land where arctic foxes live
▇ icy areas where arctic foxes live

Where Arctic Foxes Live

Arctic foxes live in the Arctic. The Arctic is a very cold area around the North Pole.

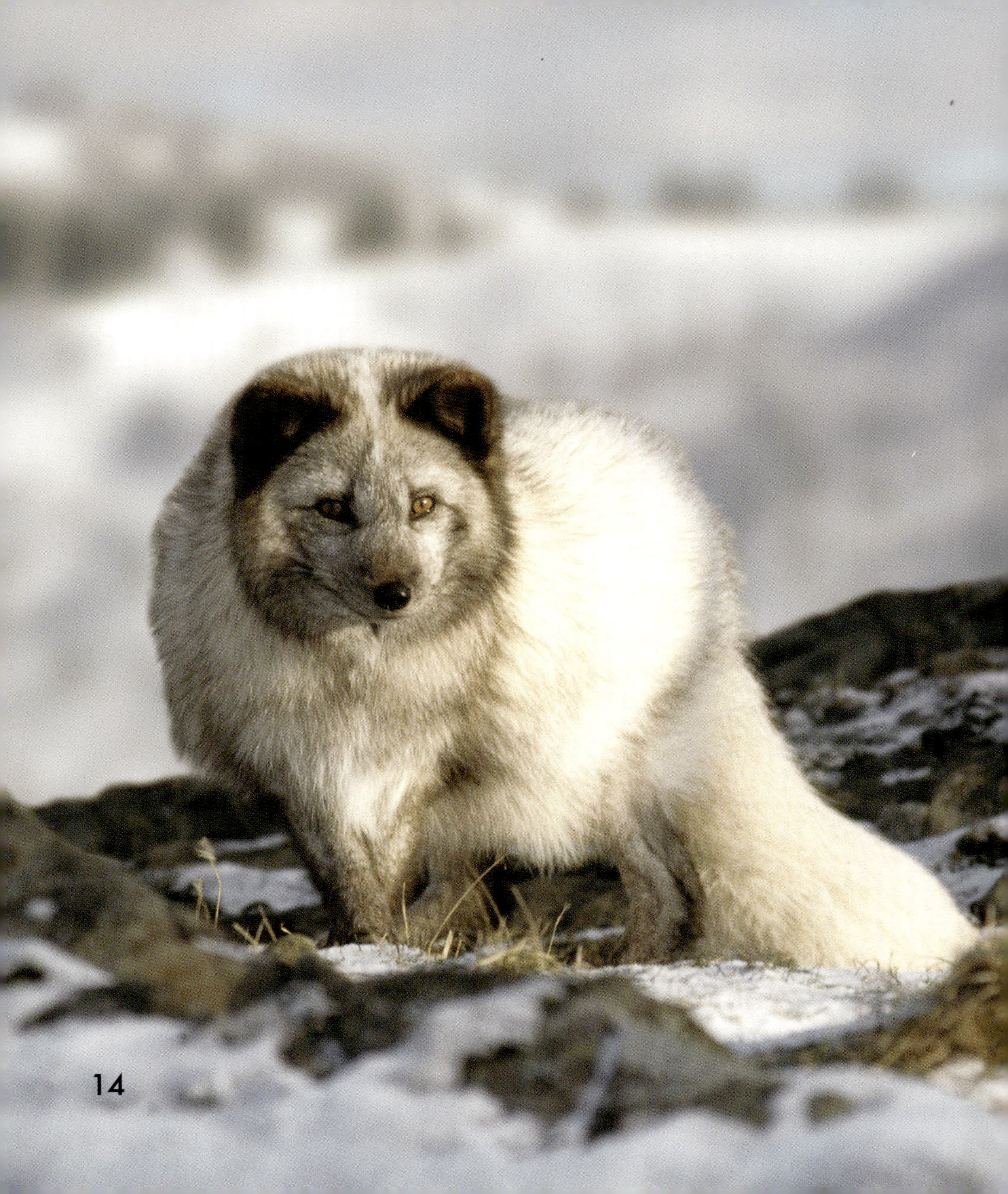

Arctic foxes live in the tundra where trees do not grow.

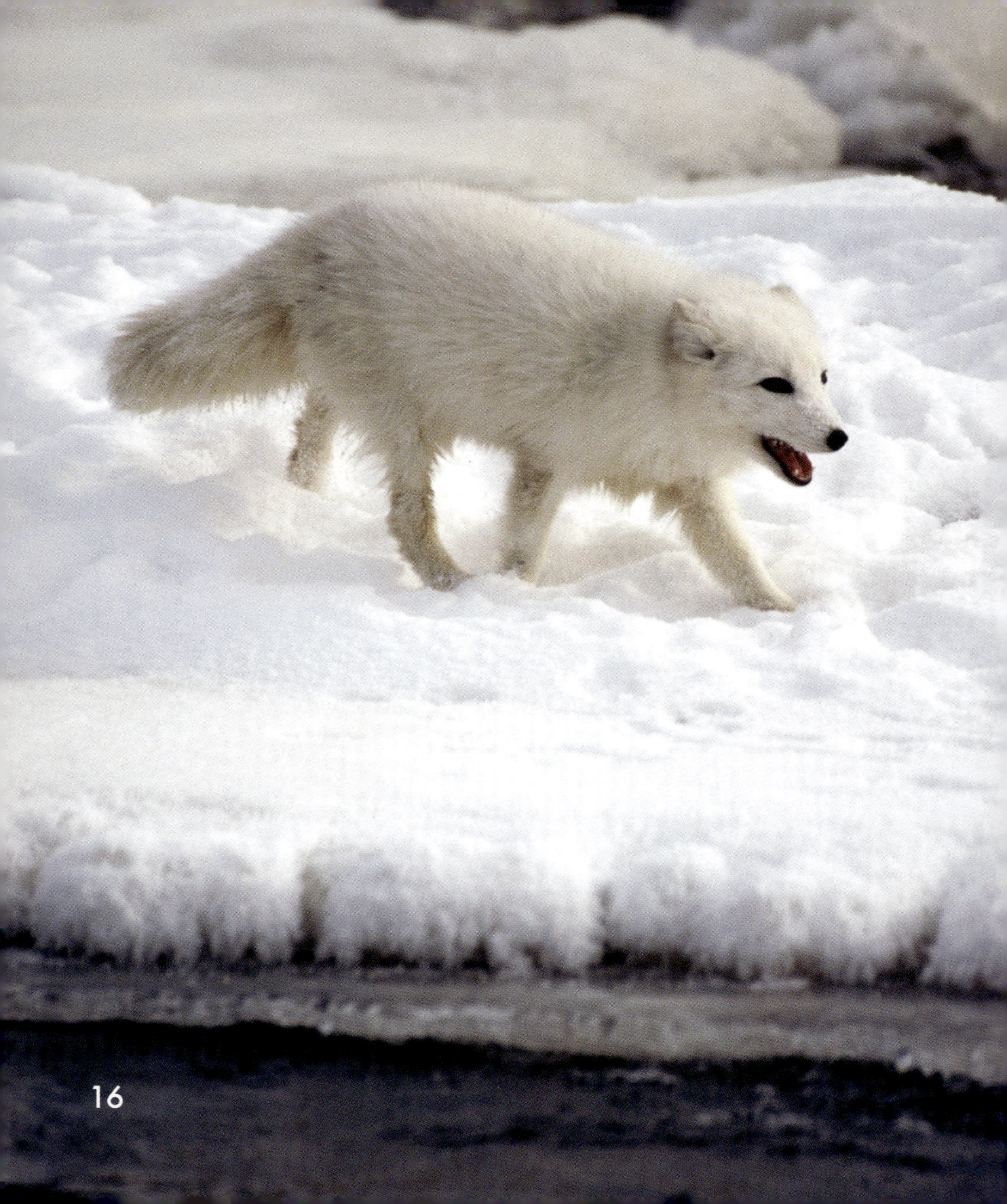

What Arctic Foxes Do

Arctic foxes hunt for food. They usually hunt alone.

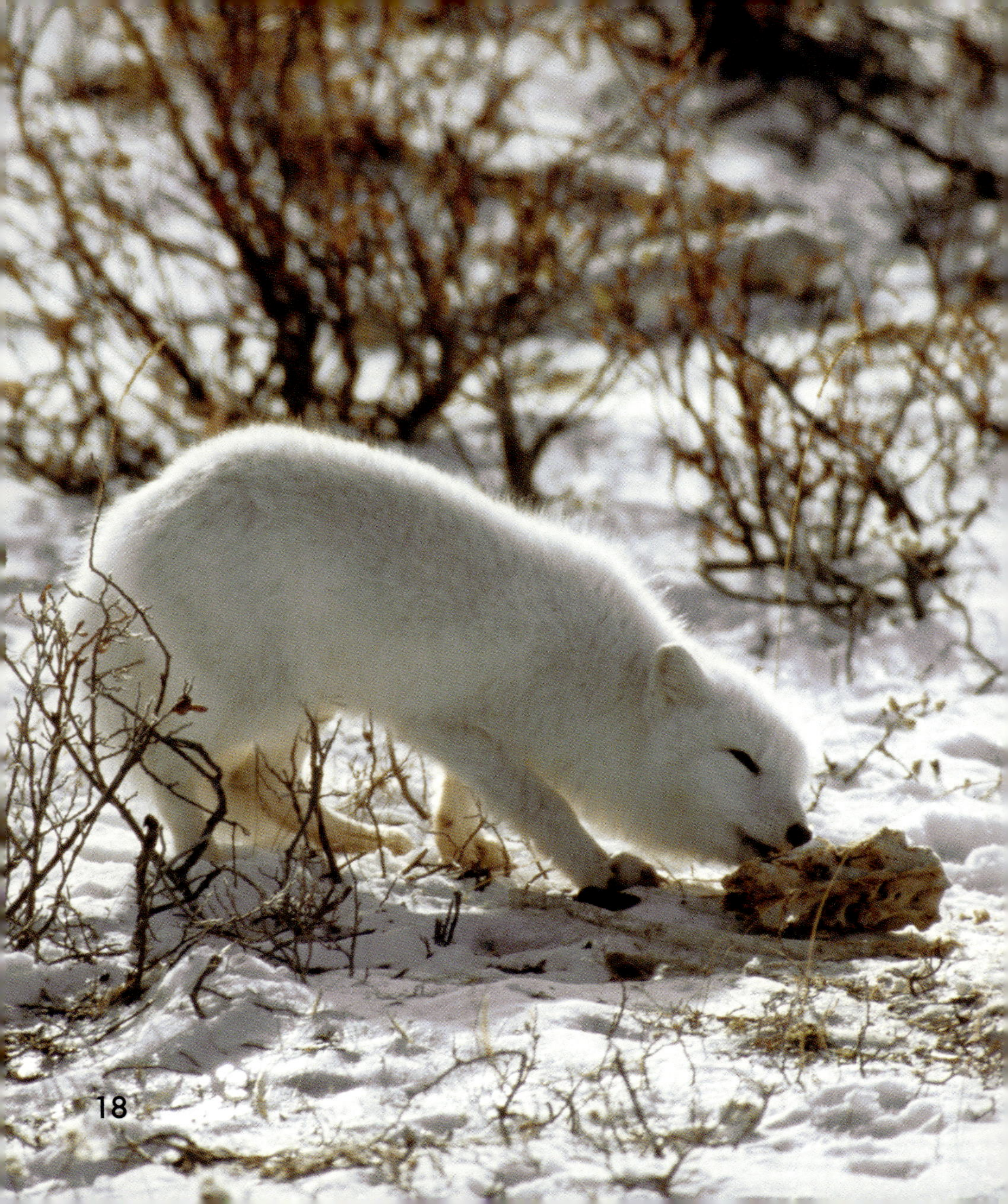

Arctic foxes eat
dead animals, lemmings,
fish, and birds.

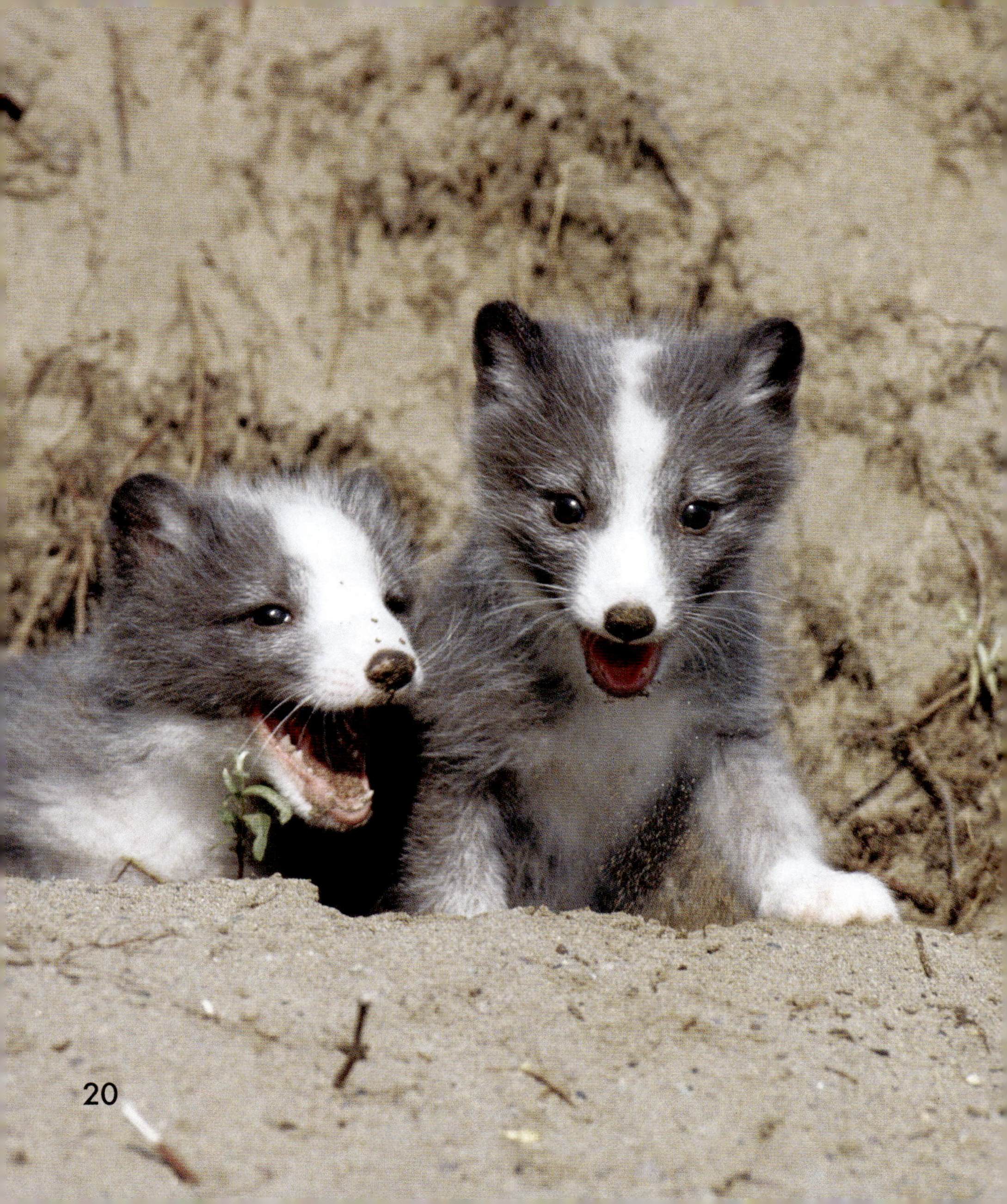

Arctic foxes dig dens to keep warm and stay safe. They live in family groups.

young arctic foxes

Glossary

Arctic—a cold region near the North Pole

bushy—thick and shaggy

den—the home of a wild animal; some arctic fox dens have been used for 300 years and can have up to 100 entrances; most dens have four to eight entrances.

lemming—a small mammal with furry feet and a short tail

mammal—a warm-blooded animal that has a backbone; a mammal has hair or fur; a female mammal feeds milk to its young.

North Pole—the northernmost point on earth; the North Pole is in the Arctic.

tundra—a cold area of northern Europe, Asia, and North America where trees do not grow; the soil under the ground in the tundra is permanently frozen.

Read More

Green, Jen. *Polar Regions.* Saving Our World. Brookfield, Conn.: Copper Beech Books, 2001.

Macken, JoAnn Early. *Polar Animals.* Animal Worlds. Milwaukee: Gareth Stevens, 2002.

Morgan, Sally. *Polar Regions.* Extreme Survival. Chicago: Raintree, 2003.

Internet Sites

FactHound offers a safe, fun way to find Internet sites related to this book. All of the sites on FactHound have been researched by our staff.

Here's how:

1. Visit *www.facthound.com*
2. Type in this special code **0736823565** for age-appropriate sites. Or enter a search word related to this book for a more general search.
3. Click on the **Fetch It** button.

FactHound will fetch the best sites for you!

Index/Word List

Arctic, 13	food, 17	sleep, 7
birds, 19	fur, 5, 9	summer, 9
brown, 9	hunt, 17	tails, 7
claws, 11	lemmings, 19	teeth, 11
cold, 13	live, 13, 15, 21	trees, 15
dens, 21		tundra, 15
dig, 21	mammals, 5	warm, 7, 21
ears, 5	North Pole, 13	white, 9
eat, 19	safe, 21	winter, 9
fish, 19	sharp, 11	

Word Count: 107
Early-Intervention Level: 13

Editorial Credits
Mari C. Schuh, editor; Patrick D. Dentinger, designer; Scott Thoms, photo researcher; Karen Risch, product planning editor

Photo Credits
Bruce Coleman Inc./Warren Photographic/Mark Taylor, 14
Corbis, cover, 12; D. Robert & Lorri Franz, 18, 20; Ron Sanford, 10
Corel, 8 (top)
Creatas, 16
Lynn M. Stone, 1, 4
PhotoDisc Inc., 6
Robin Brandt, 8 (bottom)